Heroes

in

Disguise

From Iris Schiffer
upon Mother's death
5/21/96

by LINDA PASTAN

A Perfect Circle of Sun
Aspects of Eve
The Five Stages of Grief
Waiting for My Life
PM/AM: New and Selected Poems
A Fraction of Darkness
The Imperfect Paradise

Heroes
in
Disguise

Poems by
LINDA PASTAN

W · W · NORTON & COMPANY · NEW YORK · LONDON

I would like to thank the following periodicals in which some of these poems first appeared:

The American Scholar; Antaeus; The Atlantic; Emrys; The Georgia Review; The Gettysburg Review; The Kenyon Review; Lilith; New England Review; The New Republic; The New Virginia Review; Nightsun; The Paris Review; Poetry; Ploughshares; Prairie Schooner; The Radcliffe Quarterly; Snail's Pace; The Washingtonian; Wig Wag; Yankee.

The text of this book is composed in 10/13 Gael,
with the display set in Bulmer.
Composition by ComCom division of Haddon Craftsmen, Inc.
Manufacturing by Courier Companies, Inc.

First published as a Norton paperback 1992

Library of Congress Cataloging-in-Publication Data
Pastan, Linda, 1932–
Heroes in disguise: poems / by Linda Pastan.
p.   cm.
I. Title.
PS3566.A775H47   1991
811'.54—dc20   90-25945

ISBN 0-393-30922-3

W.W. Norton & Company, Inc., 500 Fifth Avenue, New York, N.Y. 10110
W.W. Norton & Company, Ltd., 10 Coptic Street, London WC1A 1PU

2 3 4 5 6 7 8 9 0

For Oliver, Carson, Daniel,
and for Miriam Pastan

Contents

3. The Happiest Day   43

4. All We Have to Go By   61

*Hogs have been let loose
in the stubbled fields
like heroes in disguise
to find what grains of corn
are left.*

1. The Myth
of Perfectability

Autumn

I want to mention
summer ending
without meaning the death
of somebody loved

or even the death
of the trees.
Today in the market
I heard a mother say

Look at the pumpkins,
it's finally autumn!
And the child didn't think
of the death of her mother

which is due before her own
but tasted the sound
of the words on her clumsy tongue:
pumpkin; autumn.

Let the eye enlarge
with all it beholds.
I want to celebrate
color, how one red leaf

flickers like a match
held to a dry branch,
and the whole world goes up
in orange and gold.

The Way the Leaves Keep Falling

It is November
and morning—time to get to work.
I feel the little whip
of my conscience flick
as I stand at the window watching
the great harvest of leaves.
Across the street my neighbor,
his leaf blower already roaring,
tries to make order
from the chaos of fading color.
He seems brave and a bit foolish.
It is almost tidal, the way
the leaves keep falling
wave after wave to earth.

In Eden there were
no seasons, and sometimes
I think it was the tidiness
of that garden
Eve hated, all the wooden tags
with the new names of plants and trees.
Still, I am Adam's child too
and I like order, though
the margins of my poems
are ragged, and I stand here
all morning watching the leaves.

The Keeper

In Tintoretto's *Creation
of the Animals,* God
in His beard and robes extends
His great body, arms bent
like the wings of the white swan,
legs doing a kind of scissors-kick,
as if He must try flight
and swimming both, becoming Himself
part of that strange swarm—
each feather and scale and hair made
from the same new paint—
before He can declare them: Good.
It is only the fifth day.
Adam will come later
and generations later still
the keeper I remember at the Bronx Zoo
who sat among the elephants
in his gray and crumpled uniform, trumpeting
with laughter, feeding
them bits of his own lunch,
always taking the first
small taste himself.

Woman Sewing Beside a Window

"Pure and simple observation is a
deed . . ."

Edward Vuillard

He captures light
by painting its slow
diminishment: the woman
leaning over her work,
mending the flower-dark day
stitch by gathering stitch
which she will finish soon,
and fold, and put away.

The Myth of Perfectability

I hang the still life of flowers
by a window so it can receive
the morning light, as flowers must.
But sun will fade the paint,
so I move the picture to the exact center
of a dark wall, over the mantel
where it looks too much like a trophy—
one of those animal heads
but made up of blossoms.
I move it again to a little wall
down a hallway where I can come upon it
almost by chance, the way the Japanese
put a small window in an obscure place,
hoping that the sight of a particular landscape
will startle them with beauty as they pass
and not become familiar.
I do this all day long, moving
the picture or sometimes a chair or a vase
from place to place. Or else
I sit here at the typewriter,
putting in a comma to slow down
a long sentence, then taking it out,
then putting it back again
until I feel like a happy Sisyphus,
or like a good farmer who knows
that the body's work is never over,
for the motions of plowing and planting continue
season after season, even in his sleep.

Sculpture Garden

Between a bronze turtle
and a stone bird,
the wooden Adam and Eve,
carved with a chainsaw
out of old telephone poles,
stand sap-stained
in this flowerless garden,
ringed with the years
of the trees they came from
transformations ago.

I wonder if they remember
their lost leaves or the voices
that flew swifter than starlings
from telephone pole to telephone pole,
those cruciform shapes
lining the hills of the country
like stations of the cross.
It is early November.
This silence
between fall and winter

will be brief as the pause
between movements of music
when we listen
with all our attention
but may not applaud.
I think of the voices lost
since last winter. Sometimes
loneliness is so palpable
it becomes a presence
of its own, a kind of company.

Eden is lost
each time a child slides
through the torn gates
of its mother's thighs.
But here in an invented garden
I find a bestiary waiting
to be named: a wire cobra;
a turtle patient as bronze;
the stone wings of a bird
ready to fly.

December 18: for M

At the waning of the century,
with the weather warming
and even the seasons losing their way

listen to me. It is time
to sit still, to tilt your face
to the light and catch the notes of music

which sweeten the tongue
like snowflakes as they fall and melt
this bare December morning.

Your mouth was shaped for lullaby
or hymn, and your refusal
to sing bewilders

whole octaves of air. Enough
abstinence. Each day
that ends is gone, not a leaf is left

and soon enough it will be time
to sleep under the sway
of all that silence.

In the Realm of Pure Color

after Gauguin's *The Loss of Virginity*

It is our eyes that lose
their innocence, ravished by
these purples and greens as we gaze

at the woman lying there,
her ankles pressed together,
like Holbein's Christ.

She is perfectly immobile,
as if the fox signifying lust
were hardly there, nor the bird

settled on her open hand.
Even the procession that winds
its slow way towards her

is simply a curve of darkness
in the distance. In this realm
of pure color it is the intense blues

of the water that matter,
the soft shapes of the rocks,
more voluptuous than any woman.

And she becomes a flat plane of white
in the foreground, the tropical color
of sand after the sea has receded.

Topiary Gardens

"The amusement comes by each year modelling
the tree with your own shears to look more like
the bird or uncouth heraldic monster . . ."

Frances Garnet,
The Viscountess Wolseley, Gardens . . .

Was Daphne the first, twisting
into laurel as she ran, and is it a matter
of wit, or camouflage, or of rescue?

The horses in these far fields
seem made of the grass they graze on.
Escaping the knacker

they have entered a vegetable world,
a pointillist blur of bushes
where the dark beasts imagined once

outside our childhood windows
are translated benignly
into boxwood.

We could be lying in a field somewhere,
staring at the animal
shapes of clouds,

or walking past blocks of marble
in which a sculptor might see
the sentient limbs of lovers. Instead

we are here among the clipped
pyramids, the swans feathered in ivy,
the jade peacocks,

here where the gardeners
with their bright shears
replace the fates, constructing an Eden

where Eve and the snake
reflect the color of envy
in each other's eyes.

I sit at a table made of leaves
under a leafed umbrella
and look down at my own pale skin.

No moss will cover these arms,
no bright berries
that speckle the yew.

But someday,
planted deep underground,
I too will send up green shoots

to cover the hunched shoulders
of the gravestones
with a shawl of leaves.

At the Equestrian Museum

I want to be that dark woman
on horseback, gripping
the vast animal
between my knees
until I become
a part of the horse
myself, the pounding
of hoofbeats one
with the pounding
pulse in my ears,
the smell in my nostrils
nothing but horse.
I want to learn
in my bones
how a centaur can be
less myth than dream—
that old galloping dream
where I have spurs
at my ears for jewels,
my hair and the horse's tail
streaking behind
in a slipstream
of our own furious making.
I want to be more
than human flesh,
more than paint,
for this is not simply
Night Journey on Horseback
but a way of riding,
of riding the speeding
galaxy, bareback
farther and farther
from home.

The Bookstall

Just looking at them
I grow greedy, as if they were
freshly baked loaves
waiting on their shelves
to be broken open—that one
and that—and I make my choice
in a mood of exalted luck,
browsing among them
like a cow in sweetest pasture.

For life is continuous
as long as they wait
to be read—these inked paths
opening into the future, page
after page, every book
its own receding horizon.
And I hold them, one in each hand,
a curious ballast weighting me
here to the earth.

On the Marginality of Poets

At the margin of the pond,
in the live mud, there are frogs
whose whole bodies pulse,
the way the vein above
my father's eye pulsed
in thought. There are herons here,
the blue shape of flight, and small fish
whose blind seeking once
delivered all of us to land.

And on the margins of the page
it is all snow, no footfall yet.
Here is a perfect white frame
for anything, a place
where the sudden afterthought
is scrawled, or that brief star,
the asterisk. I want to live
in the margins:
those spaces neither here

nor there, like the crack
between my parents' pushed-together beds
where I used to lie; or the verge
of land between the meadow
and the woods, smooth
as the curve where a woman's
thigh and body join—
a path to the cave where life begins;
a place to watch from.

A New Poet

Finding a new poet
is like finding a new wildflower
out in the woods. You don't see

its name in the flower books, and
nobody you tell believes
in its odd color or the way

its leaves grow in splayed rows
down the whole length of the page. In fact
the very page smells of spilled

red wine and the mustiness of the sea
on a foggy day—the odor of truth
and of lying.

And the words are so familiar,
so strangely new, words
you almost wrote yourself, if only

in your dream there had been a pencil
or a pen or even a paintbrush,
if only there had been a flower.

Lost Luggage

"Dr. Magherini insists certain men and women are susceptible to swooning in the presence of great art, especially when far from home."

New York Times International Edition

Today in a palace disguised
as a museum, disguised myself
as a tourist, I entered a crucifixion scene
as part of the crowd and woke with the smell
of ancient sweat in my nostrils,
a bloody membrane over my eyes
as if I were seeing the world through
a crimson handkerchief—
they tell me I fainted.

Although I am in transit from my life,
I packed stray bits of it to take along—a comb
with relics of my graying hair, snapshots
of my own recent dead, books as thumbed
as this Bible chained to the hotel bedpost, whose verses
I read to put myself to sleep. At night
in different beds I dream of home,
but in the morning the dreams
are gone like so much lost luggage.

I know there are landscapes waiting
to be entered: forests shaded in leaf green
where winged children play on pipes;
the blue translucent scales of water in seascapes.
And on every wall are faces, gazing
through an undertow of brush strokes.
Meanwhile, framed in the evening windows
of yet another city, the woman reflected
is merely myself, the halo

of light a streetlamp shining on my head.
But ghosts clothed in tempora
follow me everywhere,
as if art itself were a purpling shadow
whose territory I must step back into,
a place where I can hide myself
over and over again, where what is lost
may be found, though always
in another language and untranslatable.

2. Only Child

Trajectory

In the trajectory
whose arc describes my life
I sense almost precisely
where I am. I see
the patchworked years
spread far below
as if this were an ordinary flight
over farms and fields
unfolding into dusk.

And it is ordinary,
ending as it must
in a single measure of earth
as other flights end,
even those of the bird
with an Indian name
whose landings are marked
by a feather pointing
towards the dark.

Autobiography in Green

1.

On the Grand Concourse,
where every tree
was in a small, wire cage,
the dog, lifting
his leg, had to imagine
the roughness of bark.

2.

And though I saw
the leaves break out in May,
one by one, obsessively
along each branch,
I wouldn't learn for years
the commonness of green.

3.

At summer camp,
I wrapped my arms around
a trunk labeled "maple"
in Gothic script,
salting the roots of that tree
for its silence, blaming,
blaming.

4.

It is all in code
what the trees say,
or illegible scrawls
of dry twig and branch.
Still I learned to watch
as they opened
those green, secret
envelopes.

5.

In the ritual battle
between wood
and fire,
how many logs
have I casually
burned, drunk
on the heraldic smell
of woodsmoke?

6.

Write of the streets
they say, of the wars
raging around you.
And I tell of the gypsy moth
brooding
in its gauzy tent,
of the helpless leaves
spreading their tethered wings.

7.

Here at last, among
dogwood,
poplar,
whole genealogies
of oak,
I grow improbably old
in my own small
commonwealth.

Only Child

Sister to no one,
I watched
the children next door
quarrel and make up
in a code
I never learned
to break.

Go play!
my mother told me.
Play! said the aunts,
their heads all nodding
on their stems,
a family of rampant
flowers

and I a single shoot.
At night I dreamed
I was a twin
the way my two hands,
my eyes,
my feet were twinned.
I married young.

In the fractured light
of memory—that place
of blinding sun or shade,
I stand waiting
on the concrete stoop
for my own children
to find me.

Unveiling

In the cemetery
a mile away
from where we used to live
my aunts and mother,
my father and uncles lie
in two long rows,
almost the way
they used to sit around
the long planked table
at family dinners.
And walking beside
the graves today, down
one straight path
and up the next,
I don't feel sad, exactly,
just left out a bit,
as if they kept
from me the kind
of grown-up secret
they used to share
back then, something
I'm not quite ready yet
to learn.

At the Air and Space Museum

When I was
nearly six my

father
opened his magic

doctor bag:
two

tongue depressors fastened by
a rubber

band;
one flick

of his hairy wrist
and lo!

we invented
flight.

Tracks

There are tracks
on this page, leading

back to a time
when trains clattered past

with the sound of typewriter keys
on one of those old machines—

an Underwood perhaps,
and words were as hard as spikes

not shadows on a screen
that might signify a plane

high up in the night,
dragging its tracks behind

in momentary ice.

Subway

Sometimes at night
I put myself
to sleep
with the names
of subway stops
between 125th
and Fordham Road: 134th . . .
145th . . . 161st . . .
The tunnel unwinds
backwards
under ruined streets
towards a room
where my mother sits
and mediates
between my need
and my father's
silence.
Childhood is cold
comfort.
The subway roars
and shakes—memory's
beast—over
its slippery tracks:
167th . . . 174th . . .
and I cling
to the loop
of numbers
as if I had an appointment
to keep,
as if my mother
and father were not
somewhere else
underground,
already asleep.

An Old Song

How loyal our childhood demons are,
growing old with us in the same house
like servants who season the meat
with bitterness, like jailers
who rattle the keys
that lock us in or lock us out.

Though we go on with our lives,
though the years pile up
like snow against the door,
still our demons stare at us
from the depths of mirrors
or from the new faces across a table.

And no matter what voice they choose,
what language they speak,
the message is always the same.
They ask "Why can't you do
anything right?" They say
"We just don't love you anymore."

The Hat Lady

In a childhood of hats—
my uncles in homburgs and derbies,
Fred Astaire in high black silk,
the yarmulke my grandfather wore
like the palm of a hand
cradling the back of his head—
only my father went hatless,
even in winter.

And in the spring,
when a turban of leaves appeared
on every tree, the Hat Lady came
with a fan of pins in her mouth
and pins in her sleeves,
the Hat Lady came—
that Saint Sebastian of pins,
to measure my mother's head.

I remember a hat of dove gray felt
that settled like a bird
on the nest of my mother's hair.
I remember a pillbox that tilted
over one eye—pure Myrna Loy,
and a navy straw with cherries caught
at the brim that seemed real enough
for a child to have to pick.

Last year when the chemicals
took my mother's hair, she wrapped
a towel around her head. And the Hat Lady came,
a bracelet of needles on each arm,
and led her to a place
where my father and grandfather waited,
head to bare head, and Death
winked at her and tipped his cap.

After the Funeral

It happened exactly
as I had imagined it would,
the ordinary colors of afternoon
becoming more than themselves—
a "bruised" sky, the "crepe"
wing of a bird, for instance—
simply because these blacks,
these purples were our own.

Birth too can be transforming
in almost this way,
our grandson's head last month
through the nursery window
no more nor less than any other—
eggs in a carton—until
we marked it: that one!
with our name.

The new child will not
fill precisely the space
that death has emptied,
though the space around the baby
expands already to fit it in.
The wheel of generations turns
with such excruciating logic,
a kind of rack to stretch us on.

During the funeral we were still
my mother's guests, eating her food
at her table. Now
that table will be divided
from its chairs,
and the tears released by such
sundering feel nearly sentimental,
a displacement of grief.

At the graveside she did not
seem to be in the box
or back at the house. I wore
her coat, the black seal
I had disapproved of, and felt her only
in my high cheekbones, my widow's peak.
You all become your mothers,
a man once told me scornfully.

We grow into our failures as well,
know ourselves finally by our imperfections.
If I could do it over I would be
more loving than she let me be,
would say goodbye more noisily.
And I would unlearn my life month by month,
year by year, until I was the new child,
hers, exactly as I am imagining.

Maria im Rosenhaag

The Virgin of the Roses
has my mother's face
in this painting stolen
then returned to the small chapel
in Colmar I visit by pure accident.
She has my mother's face.
And there is a child on her lap
who could be my infant brother, dead
in some life before my own
but never mentioned. There is a fence
of roses behind them
like the one we had behind our house—
each rose a silent, scented mouth
each thorn a memory to tempt
and tear the flesh.

It will be hard for me
to leave this church, an extra parting.
There was a girl in the Bronx
when I was growing up who heard the Virgin
call to her. "The Catholics,"
my mother said when they built a shrine
of artificial flowers there.
Now I see in Mary's plush, brocaded robe
the robes my mother wore for Sunday brunch,
and I search among the painted folds
for secrets she might have kept like handkerchiefs,
secrets beyond theology, that woman
elegant as Schongauer painted her,
stolen by death and only returned to me in dreams
and longings and here in mystery.

Letters

If I read what you once wrote,
I will want to answer in kind, to describe
for you the world as a postscript
to your life. I would tell how
the corner cabinet you left me closes
on the antique smell of home;
how the sycamore branches are so white
they could be an animal's antlers, blanched
in a moment of pure terror,
as you went white almost in a day
to signify your losses. Last week
at a museum in this southern city, I saw
the pictures John Twachtman painted
of the town where you brought me up. In them
there is a white film over everything,
as if the world were glazed in frost
even in summer. Only a pond was the clear blue
of your best china cups. It is not the way I knew
that green and leafy place,
more like seeing the known world
through the white fog that is memory
disguised as paint.
So, on my infrequent trips north
if I don't turn off the highway
when the sign says Armonk,
it is for the same reason that I don't read these letters
whose handwriting alone threatens me
with its cursive hooks and in whose blue flood
of ink I could so easefully drown.

Cousins

We meet at funerals
every few years—another star
in the constellation of our family
put out—and even in that failing
light, we look completely
different, completely the same.
"What are you doing now?"
we ask each other, "How
have you been?" At these times
the past is more palpable
than our children waiting
at home or the wives and husbands tugging
at our sleeves. "Remember . . . ?"
we ask, "Remember the time . . . ?"
And laughter is as painful
as if our ribs had secret
cracks in them.
Our childhoods remain
only in the sharp bones
of our noses, the shape
of our eyes, the way our genes call out
to each other in the high-pitched notes
that only kin can hear.
How much of memory
is imagination? And if loss
is an absence, why does it grow
so heavy? These are the questions
we mean when we ask: "Where
are you living now?" or
"How old is your youngest?"
Sometimes I feel the grief
of these occasions swell
in me until I become
an instrument in which language rises

like music. But all
that the others can hear
is my strangled voice calling
"Goodbye . . ." calling
"Keep in touch . . ."
with the kind of sound
a bagpipe makes, its bellows heaving,
and even its marching music funereal.

Yahrzeit Candle

On the second birthday
of your death
nothing
much
has changed,
though perhaps
I look less often
towards the grassy door
you left by.
The past
is a real place,
a lost and found
of days torn
off the calendar,
a littered sidewalk
where you wait
for me,
that old look
on your face—
part patience
part exasperation—
and me stuck again
in a traffic jam
of noisy
promises
and permutations.

Angels

"Are you tired of angels?"

Myra Sklarew

I am tired of angels,
of how their great wings
rustle open the way a curtain opens
on a play I have no wish to see.
I am tired of their milky robes,
their star-infested sashes,
of their perfect fingernails
translucent as shells
from which the souls
of tiny creatures have already fled.

Remember Lucifer, I want to tell them,
his crumpled bat wings
nose-diving from grace.
But they would simply laugh
with the watery sound a harp makes
cascading through bars of music.
Or they would sing to me in
my mother's lost voice,
extracting all the promises
I made to her but couldn't keep.

1932-

I saw my name in print the other day
with 1932 and then a blank
and knew that even now some grassy bank
just waited for my grave. And somewhere a gray

slab of marble existed already
on which the final number would be carved—
as if the stone itself were somehow starved
for definition. When I went steady

in high school years ago, my boyfriend's name
was what I tried out, hearing how it fit
with mine; then names of film stars in some hit.
My husband was anonymous as rain.

There is a number out there, odd or even
that will become familiar to my sons
and daughter. (They are the living ones
I think of now: Peter, Rachel, Stephen.)

I picture it, four integers in a row
5 or 7, 6 or 2 or 9:
a period; silence; an end-stopped line;
a hammer poised . . . delivering its blow.

3. The Happiest Day

Posterity

For every newborn child
We planted one live tree,
A green posterity,
So death could be beguiled
By root and branch and flower
To abdicate some power.
And we were reconciled.

Now we must move away
Leaving the trees behind
For anyone to climb.
The gold-rimmed sky goes gray.
Snow, as we turn our backs,
Obliterates our tracks.
Not even leaves can stay.

Domestic Animals

The animals in this house
have dream claws and teeth
and shadow the rooms
at night, their furled tails dangerous.
In the morning, all sweet slobber
the dog may yawn, the cat
make cat sounds deep
in its furred throat.
And who would guess
how they wait for dark
when into the green
jungle of our sleep
they insinuate
themselves, releasing
their terrible hunger.

The Happiest Day

It was early May, I think
a moment of lilac or dogwood
when so many promises are made
it hardly matters if a few are broken.
My mother and father still hovered
in the background, part of the scenery
like the houses I had grown up in,
and if they would be torn down later
that was something I knew
but didn't believe. Our children were asleep
or playing, the youngest as new
as the new smell of the lilacs,
and how could I have guessed
their roots were shallow
and would be easily transplanted.
I didn't even guess that I was happy.
The small irritations that are like salt
on melon were what I dwelt on,
though in truth they simply
made the fruit taste sweeter.
So we sat on the porch
in the cool morning, sipping
hot coffee. Behind the news of the day—
strikes and small wars, a fire somewhere—
I could see the top of your dark head
and thought not of public conflagrations
but of how it would feel on my bare shoulder.
If someone could stop the camera then . . .
if someone could only stop the camera
and ask me: are you happy?
perhaps I would have noticed
how the morning shone in the reflected
color of lilac. Yes, I might have said
and offered a steaming cup of coffee.

Hibiscus

How brazen
yet delicate is this red
hibiscus,

torn last winter
from a Florida pavement, weed
among smouldering weeds.

You wrapped it in brown paper,
hid it
under your airplane seat.

Now it trumpets
its honky-tonk
song

here
in a northern
window

and scorches
our chilly
mornings

with stolen
tropical
light.

Day Lilies

The color of rust themselves,
we plant them in clusters
by the rusted mailbox

for the unfranked messages they bring
of summer. Neither
do they spin.

Flickering briefly
on their graceful stems,
they quench

the light each evening,
folding themselves
into our rural dreams.

Sestina at 3 AM

In the imperfect dark
no hope of either love or sleep,
I listen to the wind
and water's long
bewildering dialogue, under
the common stars.

Tonight the stars
abrade the dark.
If I could under-
stand why you left, then I could sleep.
How long
until you call? No message in the wind,

not in the wind.
Braided with stars
the sky's long
awning shelters the world. And now the dark—
that first mother of sleep—
coaxes: "Go under,

let yourself go under,
let the wind
whisper you to sleep
and the stars
will go out, the dark
surf will rock you in its hammock all night long."

The night is very long.
Far under
the surface of water, dark
fish swim deaf to the wind,
only coral reefs for stars,
no need of sleep.

I want so much to sleep.
It is what I long
for, more than love. I want these tallowed stars
snuffed out under
clouds or fog. Why can't the wind
just blow them out and leave me to the dark?

sleep and sleep . . . I am going under
long and under and wind
and under . . . your face . . . the stars . . . the dark

Digital

The clock no longer
says its beads

through the quiet nights,
they have tied its hands

behind it.
And in the back rooms

of jewelry shops, watches
are being unstrapped, divided

into spools and springs and random
numbers. First they tore

the sundial down, unharnessing
shadows. They tell me

the grandfather clock in the hall
is simply lumber.

We are getting ready for infinity,
for the last swing

of the pendulum Earth
through space.

Now the only tick left
is the sound of a bullet

moving from chamber
to chamber.

Guilt

Stepchild
of the imagination,
it roams

the gardens
our mothers planted,
picking

thorned roses
for the bedsides
of the adulterers,

watering tea leaves
for the cups
of bitterness

that keep us sleepless
through the unforgiving
nights.

Camellias

I drag the lawn chair
to the center of the new lawn
where you have warned
it will ruin the delicate
grass. From here
I have a perfect view
of the pink camellia,
the one with rose-shaped flowers
which you secretly think
I have ignored. This is my camellia
viewing platform
I tell you, remembering
signposts in Japan.

You look at the dark cave
beneath my chair where the grass
will die in architectural stripes.
We look at each other.
This is one of the impasses
a marriage must
make a detour around
or else crash into.
Meanwhile the camellia
opens its flesh-colored petals
with utter unself-consciousness,
releasing its scent
into the dangerous air.

Possibilities

Today I drove past a house
we almost bought and heard
through the open window music

made by some other family.
We don't make music ourselves, in fact
we define our differences

by what we listen to.
And what we mean by family
has changed since then

as we grew larger then smaller again
in ways we knew would happen
and yet didn't expect.

Each choice is a winnowing,
and sometimes at night I hear
all the possibilities creak open

and shut like screendoors
in the wind,
making an almost musical

accompaniment
to what I know
of love and history.

Bed

In the confused nights, when I wake
shaken by dreams, sometimes
I don't know which bed I'm in
in the long procession of beds that move
like Saints' Day floats before my eyes.

Look! There's the cradle;
there's the child's narrow bed—
and beyond a doorway arched
like a church, the father and mother
breathing out their small allotment of breath.

And there's the oak four poster
where I burned all night, thinking
of the boy who had begged for hours
but wasn't allowed
between the austere sheets.

All beds are the same bed. Made fresh
each morning, they rise on their springs like loaves of bread
only to be torn apart again each night:
our futon; that Austrian featherbed; the pullman berth
that rocked us together like unborn twins.

When you first bedded me in a tangle
of silks and soft skin, I learned in my bones
of bedrock and flower beds. Years later
I know why clouds outside an airplane window comfort us
and why our youngest son embraced his mattress once

not as if it were a lover but simply itself
and said: I love you bed.
I know why they put pillows in coffins.
I know why sleep is the secret life
we hide all day, and I know where we hide it.

The Babies

Like horsechestnuts raining down
in a wind, or the pomegranates

that suddenly fill the far ditch,
the harvest of babies

has arrived, fat-cheeked,
rosy-stemmed, a whole crop

yours and ours, filling
the cribs like corncobs,

crowding the air
with the clamorous dust

of arrival: here we are,
make room, hurry up!

Balance

On the small, imaginary
kitchen scales,
I place on one side
all the scraps memory
has left me, as if I could make
a meal of them;
and on the other, all
I can surmise of the indelible
future: anniversaries,
losses. On one side I place
my mother's suede glove—
that emptied udder;

on the other the mitten
my grandson just dropped—
a woolen signpost he'll soon
outgrow. He is three;
she has been gone three years
exactly. Equilibrium is simply
that moment when the present
is as real as the past
or the future, when the air
that nourishes us
we breathe
without thinking.

4. All We Have to Go By

Dryad

I have made these woods my city,
though the fluttering of wings
and leaves, the invisible passage
of fox is the only traffic here.
Far from human habitation
I am trying to live
on beauty alone—a kind of fast,
making a virtue of hunger,
clothing myself in the precarious
colors of the trees.
The sun scatters its spoor through
the ancient underbrush, and I follow;
the light diminishes so slowly
that by the time I sleep
my eyes will be accustomed
to the mossy dark.

In This Season of Waiting

Under certain conditions,
when the moon in the western sky
seems frozen there, for instance

even as the sun is rising in the east,
so that soon two sides of the coin
will be facing each other;

or when the snow
which is a stranger here
fills our trees with its cold flowers;

when the single
bluejay at the feeder
is so still

it could be enameled there,
then the earth becomes an emblem
for whatever we believe.

All We Have to Go By

As if I had dreamed the snow
into falling,
I wake to a world
blanked out
in its particulars,
nearly erased.

This is the silence
of absolute whiteness—the mute
birds nowhere
in sight, the car
and animal tracks
filled in,

all boundaries,
as in love,
ambiguous.
Sometimes all we have
to go by
is the weather:

a message
the snow writes
in invisible ink,
what the sky means
by its litmus
colors.

Now my breath
on the chilly window
forms a cloud
which may turn to rain later,
somewhere else.

Sometimes in Winter

when I look into
the fragile faces
of those I love,

I long to be
one of those people who skate
over the surface

of their lives, scoring
the ice with patterns
of their own making,

people who have
no children,
who are attached

to earth only by
silver blades moving
at high speed,

who have learned to use
the medium of the cold
to dance in.

March 27

In this country
it snows one day
and summer comes the next,
there are no boundaries
green spreads unchecked
and under last year's leaves
the newly living and the dead
consort, as on those canvasses
of Judgment Day when weather
is finished and if God had a purpose
to his seasons, all the flowers
of heaven must answer to it.

Under the Resurrection Palm

If you eat the cabbage heart of a palm, the tree will
die . . .

In Beaufort, South Carolina, Spanish moss
hangs from the live oaks, blurring
all distinctions,
turning the landscape into a room
so filled with cobwebs
that History becomes no more
than the moment that has just passed,
and the faces lifting
from the field to watch us
could be from an engraving
we know by heart already.

Our tour guide speaks of the War
as if there had been no other,
tells us how even the Yankees
spared this hospital town
where gravestones were lifted
from the ground like doors
from their hinges to rest
the wounded Confederate soldiers on.
Hamilton, Fripp, and Barnwell
she knows their names, their houses,
which one married the other's sister.

She is as swollen with facts
as this moss which holds
twenty times its weight in water.
It is nearly silent here.
Behind the pillared porches nothing

seems to happen
except birth and death
and the barely perceptible seasons,
though sometimes drunk
on palmetto berries,
a mockingbird flies upside down.

How hard it is to believe
that the little heron
with its shy head,
the one that winters here,
is the same bird we will see
up north next summer
or that the sky which spreads
like watered silk
over this river town
is of a piece with the cold
sky at home.

Crocuses

They come
by stealth, spreading
the rumor of spring—
near the hedge . . .
by the gate . . .
at our chilly feet . . .
mothers of saffron, fathers
of insurrection, purple
and yellow scouts
of an army still massing
just to the south.

At Gettysburg

These fields can never be
simply themselves. Their green
seems such a tender green,
their contours so significant
to the tourists who stare

towards the far range of mountains
as if they are listening
to the page of history tearing
or to what they know themselves of warfare
between brothers. In this scenery

cows and cannons stand side by side
and motionless, as if they had grown here.
The cannons on their simple wheels
resemble farm carts, children
climb them. Thus function disappears almost entirely

into form, and what is left under
the impartial blue of the sky is a landscape
where dandelions lie in the tall grass
like so many spent cartridges, turning
at last to the smoke

of puffballs; where the only red
visible comes at sunset;
where the earth has grown so lovely
it seems to forgive us even as we are learning
to forgive ourselves.

Misreading Housman

On this first day of spring, snow
covers the fruit trees, mingling improbably
with the new blossoms like identical twins
brought up in different hemispheres.
It is not what Housman meant
when he wrote of the cherry
hung with snow, though he also knew
how death can mistake the seasons,
and if he made it all sound pretty,
that was our misreading
in those high school classrooms
where, drunk on boredom, we had to recite
his poems. Now the weather is always looming

in the background, trying to become more
than merely scenery, and though today
it is telling us something
we don't want to hear, it is all
so unpredictable, so out of control
that we might as well be children again,
hearing the voices of thunder
like baritone uncles shouting
in the next room as we try to sleep,
or hearing the silence of snow falling
soft as a coverlet, even in springtime
whispering: relax, there is nothing
you can possibly do about any of this.

Spring

Just as we lose hope
she ambles in,
a late guest
dragging her hem
of wildflowers,
her torn
veil of mist,
of light rain,
blowing
her dandelion
breath
in our ears;
and we forgive her,
turning from
chilly winter
ways,
we throw off
our faithful
sweaters
and open
our arms.

Laurel

I come upon
the laurel blooming
deep in the woods,

tiny fists of flowers
barely pink
among so many green leaves.

Is it
for my astonishment
it blooms

or for the deer
that come early
to feed?

Is it for the wreathmakers
searching the woods
who pause

at the hawthorne
with its bouquet
of thorns?

Ask Apollo, burly
god
of song.

Storm Warning

It sounds like gossip
what the leaves say
just as the wind runs its
great hand through them,

warning of storm.
How I fear the weather,
the random logic of watery transformations,
what the lightning may reveal.

I watch the children play
in the spaces between claps
of thunder, shaking the first raindrops
from their limbs.

And the oaks like so many
old women sway and sigh,
hiding their heads
in their green aprons.

Fall

In the fall
of the year
when the trees go back
to their essential shapes
shaking themselves
free of the clutter
of so many leaves,
I sweep my desk
clean
with the flat of my hand,
sharpen
a new pencil
and watch
for the astringent muse
who has frowned through
the murmurous summer,
who waits
for the first shock
of cold rain
on the face,
for the dogwood berries
to swell into red
on the branch
like drops of ritual
blood for the songbirds
to swallow.

October

Who can mediate
between the body and its undoing?
At night in each of my limbs
I feel the skeletal tree ache,
and I dream of leaves
in their feverish colors, floating
through the small streams
and tributaries of the blood.
At noon in the smoldering woods
I gather black grapes
that purse and caress the mouth,
I gather thistles and burrs—
whole armfuls of dissolution,
while from a branch
the chuck-will's widow calls
forgive, forgive

Boredom

"Life, friends, is boring. We must not say so."
John Berryman, Dream Song 14

In this place, though the seasons
are always changing,
the weather is always the same.
Today the underside of every leaf
looks tarnished, like the blind sides
of small oval mirrors, and there are
hundreds of them, all identical,
in which I almost see my face.
We are just passing time here,
treading in it as if it were so much water.
Now as the mercury moves
in the glass, sinking again
towards boredom, I grow afraid
thinking of Berryman
and the bridge; thinking how
I envy those curious saints who smiling
through their own reflections
say that they are never bored.
Here it is a contagion carried on the air,
like these leaves which seem to multiply
as they fall; it is an illness
for which all cures, except the last,
are temporary.

All Hallows

Leaning on a broom
I watch the children beg
from door to door
in their disguises.

I have held them
in childhood's spell,
stuffed them
with sweets,

shown them every trick
I ever knew.
Now as the season
goes up in smoke

they blow
like vagrant leaves
out of my
keeping.

Don't ask me why
I ride into the wind
or set my shriveled face
against the cold.

I have seen the pumpkin's smile
cave in. Even
the weather
has its reasons.

In Midair

This is the closest
we may get to God's voice,
this baritone pilot telling us to look

at the view, and so
obediently we look down
and there

under a featherless wing
is the world spread out
before us

in all its abstraction,
a kind of blueprint of earth,
God's first plan perhaps—

the smudges of mountain,
the thumbprints of lakes—
and all of us suspended

by an act of faith, part way
to what we think of as heaven,
and somehow alive.

Gleaning

Driving from coast
to coast down looped highways,
I notice how the future
we have been speeding towards for years
is receding behind us.
We must have crossed some boundary

and hardly noticed; people
we once hurried to greet
are standing along the roadside
waving goodbye, your grandfather
in his ancestral cap, my mother
holding aloft a flowered hanky.

Still we continue on,
the car radio playing music
we danced to
how many years ago?
When I try to count
I put myself to sleep.

"Talk to me," you say, "don't
doze off." We must watch for
whatever the stubborn flesh
still offers: the smell of hay
sharp and sweet on the air,
desire—that old song.

Look out the car window.
Hogs have been let loose
in the stubbled fields
like heroes in disguise
to find what grains of corn
are left.